Word Became Flesh

A Family Lenten Devotional Guide

*Devotions for Children and Adults
to Celebrate the Earthly Life of Christ,
His Death and Resurrection*

Written and Illustrated by Faye Maynard
Layout by Kristi Smith
Nashville, Tennessee

Preface

For many years my family has enjoyed using an Advent devotional called *The Advent Jesse Tree* by Dean Meador Lambert to prepare our hearts for Christmas. This devotional uses ornaments to be physical reminders of spiritual truths. The ladies of our church have participated in an ornament swap based on this book several times over the years. This devotional has been especially precious to our family, because when one of our sons was five years old, he made a profession of faith at Christmas as a result of our family time in the Word.

This experience showed me the life-changing influence family devotionals can have on the lives of our children. Just as it is important to prepare our hearts for Christmas, it is equally important to prepare for the celebration of Christ's death and resurrection. Unfortunately, our culture often buries the true meaning of Easter beneath the Easter Bunny, egg hunts, and candy. Many people view Lent only as a time to give up some vice or indulgence for a period of 40 days.

Several years ago, I became convinced that Lent would be a great time to do a devotional similar to *The Advent Jesse Tree*. My original draft was based on an outline in *No Ordinary Home* by Carol Brazo and included many Old Testament stories, but this draft overlapped with several of the stories in the Advent devotional. Therefore, this time I decided to focus on the earthly life of Jesus and His teachings in the gospels. There is no way to include all the wonderful accounts of Jesus' life. As John writes in John 21:25, books cannot contain all the wonderful things Jesus did and taught, I have simply chosen a balance of events and teachings that can easily be depicted in pictures or symbols and that hopefully reveal a clear message of the Gospel of God's grace through faith.

I have tried to write questions for a variety of ages. Some questions are intended to encourage the family to pull out the details from the passage. Others are designed to help apply the scriptural principles. Depending on the ages represented, choose the questions that best suit your family. Parents, I encourage you to model openness and honesty with your responses.

To create a set of ornaments I have two recommendations. One, craft your own set by creating your own 3-dimensional designs or by making photocopies of the illustrations in this guide. Secondly, I recommend that you organize a group of parents to do an ornament swap. Since there is a corresponding ornament for each day, 40 participants each choose one ornament design. Then each participant makes 40 copies of that one design. Before Ash Wednesday you gather and swap ornaments so that everyone has a set of 40 different ornaments to go with their devotional booklet.

To display your ornaments I recommend a large grapevine wreath that reminds us of a crown of thorns. Other ideas include a wooden cross with nails or hooks, a cloth-covered cross, a banner, or a ribbon to which ornaments can be pinned. Be creative and use whatever works for your family.

I have included song suggestions to add to your worship experience. Here is the link to the suggested songs, *http://gccnashville.org/wp-content/uploads/2014/02/Lenten Songsheet.pdf* where lyrics are available. "The Doxology," "Holy, Holy, Holy," and "Come Let Us Adore Him" are always good alternatives.

My prayer is that God would use this devotional guide to make His good news come alive in the minds and hearts of your whole family and make your celebration of Easter more meaningful. Christ's life, his teachings, death, and resurrection are truly such good news to a dying and suffering world.

Table of Contents

	Theme	*Symbol*
Day 30	Last Supper	a cup
Day 31	Gethsemane	a kneeling figure
Day 32	Arrest	kissing lips or sword
Day 33	Peter's Denial	a rooster
Day 34	Trail and Sentencing	crown of thorns or dice
Day 35	Crucifixion	a cross
Day 36	Burial	a tear drop or herbal sachet
Day 37	Resurrection	an empty tomb or shroud
Day 38	Appearing to Disciples	a hand with a scar
Day 39	Miraculous Catch	a full net of fish
Day 40	Ascension	a cloud

Day 1 – Birth of Jesus

Scripture – Luke 2:1-20

Symbol – a manger or a star

Songs – "Away in a Manger," "Silent Night," "Immanuel," "Joy to the World"

Questions

1. Why did Mary and Joseph go to Bethlehem?
2. Where was Jesus born? What were the circumstances?
3. How did people learn that something special had happened in Bethlehem?
4. How did the angels describe Jesus?
5. How did Mary respond to the things that happened? How did the shepherds respond?
6. How will you respond to the things that happened in this story?

Prayer

Jesus, give us faith to believe You are the Christ, the Savior of the world and our own souls. It is truly amazing that as God, You became a baby and lived in our world. Like the shepherds may we rejoice in Your coming, and may we spread the good news to others. It is truly good news for all the peoples. Glory to God in the highest! Amen.

Day 2 – Temple Presentation

Scripture – Luke 2:21-40

Symbol – a baby

Songs – "Praise Him, Praise Him, All Ye Little Children," "Tell Me the Story of Jesus," "When Love Came Down (to earth...)"

Questions

7. How did Jesus get his name?

8. Why did Mary and Joseph take Jesus to Jerusalem? What did they do there?

9. Who was Simeon, and what did he say about Jesus? Why was the idea that the Christ was for all peoples, including the Gentiles, surprising to people in the Bible?

10. How did Jesus' parents react to what they were told? What do you think about Simeon's words?

11. Who else thanked God and spoke about Jesus?

12. What else did you learn about Jesus' childhood?

Prayer

Lord, I pray that like Simeon and Anna, we would be seeking You with all our hearts and looking for Your promises to be fulfilled. Fill us with Your Holy Spirit that we would see things through Your eyes and understand how You are at work around us. Give us eyes to see and faith to believe Your truth. Thank You that salvation comes through faith in Jesus, both for Jews and Gentiles. Amen.

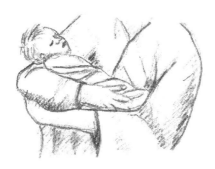

Day 3 – Visit of the Magi

Scripture – Matthew 2:1-12

Symbol – a gift or gold

Songs – "We Three Kings," "Come, Thou Long Expected Jesus,"
"O Come, O Come Emmanuel," "O Come, All Ye Faithful,"
"O Little Town of Bethlehem"

Questions

13. What were the Magi seeking, and where did they come from?
14. Where was the Christ to be born? What does the prophesy in Micah 5:2 say about Him?
15. What did Herod ask the Magi to do? Did Herod really want to worship the child?
16. What was the Magi's response to seeing the star and the child?
17. How did they worship Jesus?
18. How did God protect Jesus from Herod?
19. The Magi worshiped Jesus by bowing down and giving him gifts. How can you worship Him?
20. What is your response to Jesus coming to earth in the form of a baby and dwelling among us?

Prayer

Like the Magi, may we have hearts that seek You so earnestly that we are willing to go to great lengths: sacrificing time, effort, money, etc., to believe, trust, and worship You. May we understand that our tithes, gifts, and offerings are acts of worship, expressing our love and appreciation for Your gift of Jesus and our salvation through Him. Amen.

Day 4 – Boyhood in Egypt

Scripture – Matthew 2:13-23

Symbol – a pyramid

Songs – "Heavenly Father," "Do Not Fear (I Am the Lord Your God)"

Questions

1. How was Joseph warned to leave Bethlehem?
2. What was Joseph told to do?
3. How did Jesus' family leave and where did they go?
4. What did Herod do to try to kill Jesus and thwart God's plan?
5. When and how did Jesus' family move to Nazareth?
6. Like Joseph, is there something that your think God wants you to do that may be difficult, but that may be used for your deliverance?
7. How does God expect us to obey?

Prayer

Lord, thank You for protecting Jesus from Herod's wicked scheme. We are so comforted to know that You are always in control of our circumstances no matter how desperate. Your plans can never be stopped. Help us to be like Joseph, who recognized Your leading and obeyed Your instruction immediately and without question. Amen.

Day 5 – Visit to the Temple

Scripture –Luke 2:41-52; 1 Timothy 4:12

Symbol – a scroll, Bible, or the temple

Songs – "B-I-B-L-E, Is the Book for Me," "Thy Word," "Father, I Adore You"

Questions

1. How did Jesus and His family celebrate the Feast of Passover every year? How old was Jesus in this story?

2. What happened when Mary and Joseph left Jerusalem?

3. Where did they find Jesus, and what was He doing? How did people react to His knowledge of God's Word?

4. What explanation did Jesus give for His actions, and what did He call the temple?

5. From verses 51 and 52, what else do we learn about Jesus' youth?

6. Read 1 Timothy 4:12. How does this verse relate to this story about Jesus' youth? How should we be an example to others?

7. How well do you know God's word? How can you know it better?

Prayer

Jesus, may we be like You, hiding God's Word in our hearts at an early age: studying it and asking questions to understand God's instructions. Thank You that by faith we can also call the God of the universe our "Father". Like You, may we be obedient and may we grow in favor with both our Heavenly Father and other people. Amen.

Day 6 – Baptism of Jesus

Scripture – Matthew 3; Galatians 5:22
Symbol – a dove and/or water
Songs – "Spirit of God," "Spirit of the Living God,"
Questions

1. What was John the Baptist preaching, and how were the people responding? What does it mean to be "repentant"?
2. Describe John.
3. How did John rebuke the corrupt religious leaders who came to watch? What did he tell them they needed to do?
4. What does it mean for people to bear "good fruit"? Read Galatians 5:22.
5. John baptized with water, but what did he say about the One who was coming? How will He baptize?
6. How did John respond to Jesus' request to be baptized in water? Why did Jesus say He needed to be baptized?
7. What happened when Jesus came out of the water?
8. If you have repented of your sins and believe that Jesus' blood has covered your sin, talk as a family about when you might consider expressing your faith through being baptized.

Prayer

Lord, your kingdom is near. May we see our sin, ask for forgiveness, turn from our sin, and bear good fruit. It truly is Your kindness that leads us to repentance. Thank You for the Holy Spirit, who makes it possible for us to bear good fruit. Amen.

Day 7 – Christ's Temptation

Scripture – Matthew 4:1-11; Ephesians 6:10-18

Symbol – a cactus or stones

Songs – "Oh Be Careful Little Eyes What You See," "All Hail the Power of Jesus' Name," "You Are My Hiding Place," "Whom Have I in Heaven but Thee," "Before the Throne of God Above"

Questions

1. What prepared Jesus for his time in the desert?
2. What does it mean to "fast"?
3. How did Satan tempt Jesus when He was hungry? How did Jesus respond?
4. How did Satan tempt Jesus to test God? How did Jesus respond?
5. How did Satan tempt Jesus to worship him? Again how did Jesus respond?
6. What happened when Jesus endured all the temptations?
7. When and how does Satan tempt you?
8. Read Ephesians 6:10-18. What is our weapon and protection against spiritual temptations and attacks?

Prayer

Lord, prepare us for times when we are tempted. Help us to rely on Your Word and use it like a sword in battle against our sin and the devil's schemes. Like Jesus, may we be faithful in prayer and clothed in Your armor to help us stand firm. Amen.

Day 8 – Calling of Disciples

Scripture – Luke 5:1-11

Symbol – a net or a boat

Songs – "Fishers of Men," "I Have Decided to Follow Jesus," "I Will Live My Life for Him," "I Will Change Your Name"

Questions

1. What was Jesus doing by the Lake of Gennesaret (Sea of Galilee)? How did Simon Peter help Jesus?

2. Once Jesus had finished speaking to the crowd, what did He tell the fishermen to do?

3. What did Simon call Jesus? What does this tell us about who he believed Jesus to be?

4. What happened when the fishermen obeyed Jesus' instruction?

5. How did Simon Peter respond? Why do you think he says for Jesus to go away from him?

6. What did Jesus tell the fishermen they will be? How did they respond? How would you respond?

7. What does it mean to be "fishers of men"? How can you tell others about Jesus?

Prayer

Jesus, as You did for Simon Peter, give us eyes to see that You are God, Lord, and Messiah. You are worthy of our obedience and devotion. Thank You for giving us a new calling and purpose. Thank You for letting us follow You and spread the good news. Amen.

Day 9 – First Miracle

Scripture – John 2: 1-11

Symbol – 2 wedding rings or large jugs

Songs – "Wonderful, Merciful Savior," "Immanuel" (chorus),
   "He Is Good"

Questions

1. What event in Cana did Jesus, His mother, and disciples attend?
2. What problem arose that Mary expected Jesus to help fix?
3. How did Jesus help? What did Jesus tell the servants to do?
4. What happened to the water?
5. How did the master of the banquet describe the wine?
6. What was the result of this sign? What effect do the stories of Jesus' miracles have on your faith?

Prayer

Lord, thank You for caring about the concerns and problems of people and helping us in our distress. We also rejoice in Your approval of marriages and Your beautiful design for families. Thank You for displaying Your glory in this story so that we, like the disciples, can have greater faith in You. Amen.

Day 10 – Feeding of 5000

Scripture – Mark 6:30-44

Symbol – bread and fish

Songs – "My Shepherd," "Give Thanks," "Come Worship the Lord,"
"How Much More," "Jesus I Am Resting, Resting"

Questions

1. Why did Jesus and the disciples go to a solitary place? What did Jesus realize His disciples needed?
2. What happened when they got to the solitary place?
3. What needs did Jesus see among the people, and how did He respond?
4. What was the disciples' solution to the people's hunger and why?
5. What was Jesus' solution? What did He instruct the disciples to do? What was the result?
6. What does this miracle teach us about Jesus? What can we learn about how to meet overwhelming needs?

Prayer

Lord, thank You for Your compassion for our weaknesses and our needs for rest and food, as well as spiritual leadership and guidance. We are truly lost sheep in need of a Good Shepherd to lead and provide for our most basic needs, both physical and spiritual. Instead of being overwhelmed by the needs of the world, may we pray for Your provision and be generous and faithful with what You have given. In You we can find rest and nourishment. Amen.

Day 11 – Prayer

Scripture – Matthew 6:5-15

Symbol – praying hands

Songs – "If You Abide in Me," "What a Friend We Have In Jesus,"
"Tender Mercy," "The Lord's Prayer"

Questions

1. What is a "hypocrite"? What did Jesus say the hypocrites were doing wrong when they prayed?

2. What instruction did Jesus give the disciples about how to pray? Do you have a place you pray in secret?

3. Is God surprised by anything we pray?

4. To follow Jesus' sample prayer, who should we praise? What should we hope and have faith will happen? What should we request?

5. What did you learn about forgiveness? Why is it so important to forgive others?

6. Is there anyone you have not forgiven? What do you think God wants you to do in that situation?

Prayer

Lord, we want to praise and honor Your name. We pray for Your kingdom to spread throughout all the earth and Your will to be done so that Christ can return in glory. May we trust You for our daily needs and forgive other people because we are also in great need of Your forgiveness. Lastly, guard our hearts from temptation and give us the strength to flee tempting situations, and please protect us from evil. Amen.

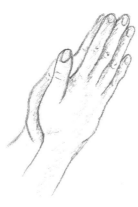

Day 12 – Woman at the Well

Scripture – John 4:1-42

Symbol – a well or bucket

Songs – "Spring Up, O Well," "Deep and Wide," "Antiphonal Praise
(We Worship You, Almighty God)," "Psalm 9 (I Will Praise)"

Questions

1. On Jesus' journey to Galilee, where did He stop to rest?
2. Why was the Samaritan woman surprised that Jesus asked her for a drink?
3. What did He say He could give her? What did Jesus mean by "living water"?
4. How do true worshipers worship God? How do you worship your heavenly Father?
5. Who did Jesus claim to be? Why was telling a Samaritan about Himself important? Who does God want to hear the gospel message?
6. What did Jesus say is His food?
7. What did the woman do after talking with Jesus? How do you respond to the good news of the Gospel?

Prayer

Jesus, thank You for loving all people and for wanting them to know that You are the Messiah. Only in You can our thirst for truth be satisfied. May we worship You in spirit and truth and share what we have learned with our friends, family, and others. Amen.

Day 13 – Do Not Worry

Scripture – Matthew 6:25-34; Philippians 4:6-7

Symbol – a bird or a lily

Songs – "Seek Ye First," "Be Still and Know," "Like a River Glorious," "It Is Well With My Soul"

Questions

1. What were the worries of the people whom Jesus was teaching? What are you worried about?
2. Why did He say we should not worry about food, drink, or clothes?
3. When we worry, what does it show that we lack?
4. What examples did He give of God's provision? What examples can you give of God's provision in your life?
5. What did Jesus say about our worth in God's eyes?
6. What will be the result when we seek His kingdom first?
7. Instead of worrying, what should we do? Read Philippians 4:6-7.

Prayer

Lord, You know we struggle with worrying about things in our lives. Forgive our lack of faith in Your love and provision. Instead of focusing on our needs and wants, help us to keep our eyes on You and Your kingdom. We thank You that You know our needs and that You are faithful to provide. May we bring our concerns to You and be content and satisfied in You. Amen.

Day 14 – Jesus Walks on the Water

Scripture – Matthew 14:22-33

Symbol – a man walking on water

Songs – "Trust and Obey," "Indescribable," "Jesus, I Am Resting, Resting"

Questions

1. After Jesus sent the disciples to the other side of the lake, what did He do?
2. Why did Jesus need time alone?
3. What was happening to the disciples in the boat?
4. How did Jesus come to them? Why were they so afraid?
5. What proof did Peter ask from Jesus?
6. What happened to Peter when he trusted Jesus? What happened when he focused on the danger and his own fears?
7. What do you fear? What does this story teach us about how to face our fears?
8. What happened when Jesus and Peter entered the boat?
9. How did this miracle affect the disciples? Who do you believe Jesus to be?

Prayer

Jesus, if You needed time alone to pray, how much more do we need to spend time with You in prayer. Help us to make time for You in our lives. When we are afraid and in danger, may we look to You and trust that You are watching over us. Also, may our faith grow as we understand more about You and trust You more. Amen.

Day 15 – Faith

Scripture – Matthew 8:5-13; Matthew 17:20; Ephesians 2:8-10

Symbol – a mustard seed or mountain

Songs – "God Said It," "My Faith Has Found a Resting Place,"
"It's By Grace," "'Tis So Sweet"

Questions

1. In Matthew 8, why did the centurion come to Jesus?
2. What did the centurion believe Jesus could do?
3. Why was Jesus astonished by the centurion's faith?
4. What do we learn from this story about who can have faith? Who does Jesus say will be at God's feast in the kingdom of heaven?
5. What happened to the servant?
6. From Matthew 17:20, if we have a little faith, what can we do?
7. What "mountain" do you need moved in your life?
8. Read Ephesians 2:8-10. How do we get faith?
9. What is the result of faith?

Prayer

Lord, give us the gift of faith that we may be saved from our sin by Your grace. We confess our faith is often small. Help us to trust and have faith in Your great power to do big things. We thank You that faith is not limited to one race of people, but like the centurion, all who believe may enter Your kingdom. As a result of believing, may we faithfully do the good works You have prepared for us. Amen.

Day 16 – Healing the Lame

Scripture – Luke 13:10-17; John 5:1-15

Symbol – a crutch or mat

Songs – "Walking and Leaping and Praising God," "Blessed Be Your Name (in a land that is plentiful)"

Questions

1. In Luke 13:10-17, what was wrong with the woman and how did Jesus heal her?
2. Why was the synagogue ruler upset by Jesus healing her?
3. How did Jesus defend His actions? Why did He call Jewish leaders "hypocrites"?
4. What was the reaction of the people present? How do you react to Jesus' actions and teachings?
5. In John 5:1-15, what did Jesus ask the invalid? What did Jesus tell him to do?
6. Why did the Jews get upset with the man after he was healed? How should we observe the Sabbath?
7. Later when Jesus saw the man again, what did He tell him? What can we learn from this warning?

Prayer

Jesus, we thank You for having compassion on those who are suffering. Give us a heart for them as well. May we learn to rest and observe the Sabbath without using it as an excuse to neglect doing good deeds and caring for others. Lord, since You have healed us from our sins, may we walk in a manner worthy of Your calling and not return to our old sinful ways. Amen.

Day 17 – Parables of Treasure and Pearl

Scripture – Matthew 13:44-46; Philippians 3:7-9
Symbol – a pearl or treasure box
Songs – "More Precious than Silver," "Great Is the Lord"
Questions

1. In Matthew 13:44, to what is the kingdom of heaven compared?
2. How did the man respond when he found the treasure? Are you willing to dig in God's word and see its true value in your life?
3. What is the kingdom of heaven worth to you? Although we can do nothing to buy or earn salvation, there is a cost of discipleship. What are you willing to give or sacrifice to believe and follow Jesus?
4. In Matthew 13:45-46, what was the merchant doing? What did he do when he found the pearl? Are you searching for truth, and what is it worth to you?
5. Read Philippians 3:7-9. What things did you trust in before you knew Jesus? How do those things compare to knowing Christ?

Prayer

Lord, thank You for the great riches in Christ: a relationship with our heavenly Father, forgiveness of our sin, a transformed life, and an eternal hope. These great treasures, which are ours when we believe, are truly of priceless worth. May we value our salvation greatly and gladly pay the cost of discipleship. Amen.

Day 18 – Healing the Blind

Scripture – Mark 10:46-52
Symbol – an eye, eye patch, or glasses
Songs – "Be Thou My Vision," "Open Our Eyes"
Questions

1. Where was Jesus in this story, and what was He doing?
2. Who was Bartimaeus, and what was his need?
3. What did he do when he heard Jesus was passing by?
4. What did he call Jesus? Although he was physically blind, what does this reveal about what he saw clearly?
5. How did Bartimaeus respond to Jesus' calling? How are you responding to Jesus' calling?
6. What did Jesus say has healed Bartimaeus?
7. What did Bartimaeus do after he was healed? How is your life changed from responding in faith to Jesus?

Prayer

Jesus, we are all spiritually blind and need healing to see Your true identity. Like Bartimaeus, may we come running to You in love and in faith. May our lives be transformed, and may we joyfully follow You. Amen.

Day 19 – Sign of Jonah

Scripture – Matthew 12:38-42

Symbol – a whale or big fish

Songs – "Grace Flows Down (and covers me)," "Near the Cross," "Whale Did Swallow Jonah"

Questions

1. What were the Jewish leaders asking from Jesus?
2. What did Jesus call them? Why?
3. What is the sign of Jonah? What was Jesus predicting?
4. Why did He say that the men of Ninevah will stand in judgment over this generation? Are you repentant like the Ninevites or are You more like the Jewish leaders?
5. What was the Queen of the South seeking from Solomon? Why will she condemn this generation?
6. Who is the One greater than Jonah and Solomon that this passage is talking about?
7. What was Jesus' greatest miraculous sign?

Prayer

Help us to examine our own hearts. What are we really seeking? May we earnestly seek Your truth and Your wisdom. When we hear You, may we respond with truly repentant hearts. May we turn from our sinful ways and by the power of Your Holy Spirit walk in Your righteousness. Amen.

Day 20 – Transfiguration

Scripture – Matthew 17:1-13

Symbol – a sun for God's glory

Songs – "Glory, Glory to the King," "The Lamb is Worthy (echo song),"
   "Holy, Holy, Holy"

Questions

1. Which disciples were with Jesus on the mountain?
2. What happened to Jesus on the mountain? What did He look like?
3. Who else appeared talking with Jesus?
4. What did the voice from the cloud say? What does this prove about Jesus' identity?
5. How did the disciples respond?
6. What instruction did Jesus give them? When could they tell others this story?
7. What did Jesus say about Elijah coming? What happened to Elijah when he came? Who did the disciples understand that He was talking about?
8. What did Jesus say will happen to the Son of Man? Who is the Son of Man?

Prayer

Heavenly Father, we thank You for affirming Jesus' identity to the disciples so that we could have their witness in Your Word. Jesus, You truly are the sinless Son of God. Thank You for coming and suffering on our behalf. We long for You to return in glory. Amen.

Day 21 – Parable of the Sower

Scripture – Luke 8: 1-15

Symbol – seeds, rocks, thorns, or soil

Songs – "Change My Heart, Oh God," "Holiness Is My Desire"

Questions

1. Who traveled with Jesus as He was proclaiming the good news of the kingdom of God? How did the women support His ministry? How can you use what you have to support Christ's ministry?

2. In the parable Jesus tells, name the kinds of soils.

3. In Jesus' explanation of the parable:

   What is the seed?

   What does the path represent?

   What does the rocky soil represent?

   What does the soil with thorns represent?

   What does the good soil represent?

4. What kind of soil is in your heart? How do you receive the Word of God? What "crops" do you see in your life?

Prayer

Lord, we pray for a noble heart of good soil where Your Word takes root and grows. Please protect us from the evil one and from being choked by life's worries, riches, and pleasures. By Your strength may we bear an abundant crop of good fruit. Amen.

Day 22 – Zacchaeus

Scripture – Luke 19:1-10

Symbol – a sycamore leaf

*Songs – "Zacchaeus Was a Wee Little Man," "Jesus Is All the World
to Me (He's my friend)," "Create In Me a Clean Heart,"
"Greatest End"*

Questions

1. Who was Zacchaeus? What do you think is unusual about a wealthy chief tax collector climbing a tree to see Jesus?
2. Are you willing to look foolish in the eyes of the world to seek Jesus? What lengths will you go to in order to learn more about Jesus and His message?
3. What did Jesus say to Zacchaeus? How did Zacchaeus receive Jesus in his home?
4. Jesus is knocking at your door. How will you receive Him?
5. How did Zacchaeus change as a result of hearing Jesus' message?
6. How has your life changed as a result of knowing Jesus?
7. What did Jesus say had happened to Zacchaeus?
8. Why did the Son of Man come?

Prayer

Jesus, thank You for coming to seek and save the lost because we are all sinners and lost without You. May we do whatever it takes to learn more about You, particularly not worrying about what other people think about us. May we be more concerned about pleasing You than other people. If we have wronged others, show us how best to make amends. Amen.

Scripture – Luke 15:11-32

Symbol – a pig or nice robe

Songs – "Come Ye Sinners Poor and Needy," "Father, I Adore You,"

Questions

1. What did the younger son demand from his father? How would you describe the younger son?
2. Where did his selfish sinful living lead him?
3. Why did he return home?
4. How did the father react to his return? How would you describe the father? Who loves us this way?
5. How did the older brother react to his brother's return? How would you describe the older brother?
6. Which brother are you more like?
7. What is Jesus' message in this parable?

Prayer

Lord, we confess that we live selfishly and sinfully. At times we dishonor and reject You and Your love. At other times, we are like the older brother who is hard-working but is serving out of duty, not love, and who is judgmental of others. This too is sinful. Please forgive us. Father, thank You for seeking us and welcoming us back into Your arms and forgiving our sin. Thank You for rejoicing over every sinner who repents. Amen.

Day 24 – The Raising of Lazarus

Scripture – John 11:1-44

Symbol – a man wrapped in white

Songs – "I Am the Resurrection," "You Are My All in All,"
   "In Christ Alone"

Questions

1. Who were Lazarus' sisters? How did Jesus feel about Lazarus and his sisters?
2. What reason did Jesus give for why Lazarus was sick?
3. What did Jesus call Himself in verse 25?
4. What did Jesus say about anyone who believes in Him?
5. How did Jesus feel as He saw the family and friends mourning Lazarus' death? What did Jesus do for Lazarus?
6. What reason did Jesus give for doing this miracle?
7. Do you believe that God sent Jesus and that by believing in Him you may have eternal life?
8. If we believe that there is eternal life and that Jesus grants it to those who believe, how will that affect our view of death and how we live?

Prayer

Lord, You are the resurrection and the life. Thank You for conquering death through Your sacrifice on the cross. For those who believe in You, although we will die physically, we praise You that we will be raised with You in glory. Jesus, thank You for displaying Your resurrection power so that we might believe in You. Amen.

Day 25 – Triumphal Entry

Scripture – Matthew 21:1-11; Philippians 3:20-21; 1 Peter 2:9-10
Symbol – a palm branch or donkey
Songs – "Hosanna," "Hosanna in the Highest," "Glory, Glory to the King," "The King Has Come," "Jesus Shall Reign"
Questions

1. What did Jesus send two disciples to do in the village?
2. In times of peace it was a tradition for the king to ride on a donkey. From Zechariah 9:9, what was the significance of Jesus entering Jerusalem riding on a donkey colt?
3. The people expected the Messiah to be a king to set them free from the tyranny of Rome, but instead what kind of peace does Jesus bring?
4. How did the crowd greet Jesus?
5. "Hosanna" is an expression of adoration meaning "oh, save". From what do we need saving?
6. Read Philippians 3:20-21. As believers, where is our citizenship, and what will happen in our future?
7. Read 1 Peter 2:9-12. How are the people of God described? Because we are called to be a holy people how should we live?

Prayer

Hosanna! Please save us! We desperately need you to save us from our sin. We are so thankful that You came offering salvation and peace with God. May we rejoice in being part of Your kingdom and being called by Your name. Amen.

Day 26 – Cleansing of the Temple

Scripture – Mark 11:15-19

Symbol – a whip, coins, or temple

Songs – "Holy, Holy, Holy," "What a Friend We Have in Jesus,"
  "Lord Most High"

Questions

1. What did Jesus do when He entered the temple? Why did Jesus stop the merchants and money changers?
2. What did He teach is the purpose of the temple?
3. According to Isaiah 56:7, who was encouraged to worship God in the temple?
4. What is the purpose of going to church?
5. Why did the chief priests and teachers of the law want to kill Jesus?
6. How did the crowd react to His teaching? How do you react to His teaching?

Prayer

Lord, help us to focus on You in worship and prayer. Forgive us when we are distracted by pleasing other men and meeting their expectations. Thank You that people from all nations are welcome at Your throne and altar. May we delight in coming before You in prayer. Amen.

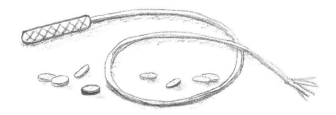

Day 27 – Anointing of Jesus

Scripture – John 12:1-11

Symbol – a small bottle or beaded box

Songs – "Fairest Lord Jesus," "I Love You, Lord"

1. Where was Jesus, and who else was there?
2. What did Mary do, and why do you think she did this?
3. Why did Judas Iscariot object to Mary's extravagance? What pretense did Judas use to try to cover his greed?
4. How do you attempt to cover your sin?
5. How did Jesus defend Mary's actions?
6. Imagine yourself at that dinner. What would you see, smell, hear, and feel?
7. Why did a large crowd gather? Why did the chief priests make plans to kill Jesus and Lazarus? Of what were they afraid?

Prayer

Like Mary may we love You, Lord, so much that we are willing to give You all we have and lavish You with love and praise. Unlike Judas, may we identify our sin and confess it rather that attempting to cover it with a pretense or mask of righteousness. Amen.

Day 28 – Judas' Plot

Scripture – Matthew 26:1-4, 14-25; Matthew 6:19-24
Symbol – a bag of silver coins
Songs – "More Precious than Silver," "As the Deer"
Questions

1. In Matthew 26:1-4, what did Jesus know was going to happen to Him?
2. What were the Jewish leaders plotting?
3. In Matthew 26:14-16, who went to the chief priests? What did he ask them? What deal did they make?
4. Judas loved money more than Jesus. What are you tempted to love more than Jesus?
5. In Matthew 26:20-25, at the Last Supper what did Jesus say about the one who would betray Him?
6. Read Matthew 6:19-24. Where is your treasure? What are the two masters that cannot both be served? How does the love of money creep into your heart and express itself?

Prayer

Lord, guard our hearts from the love of money or any other form of idolatry that would steal our love from You. Jesus, although You knew You would be betrayed by one of Your own disciples and that you would be crucified, You courageously did the Father's will. Thank You for Your great love, faithfulness, and sacrifice. Amen.

Scripture – John 13:1-17

Symbol – a towel and/or basin

Songs – "They Will Know We Are Christians by Our Love,"
"Beautiful, Scandalous Night," "Nothing But the Blood"

Questions

1. At the Passover Feast, what did Jesus do to demonstrate His love to the disciples?
2. The passage tells us that Jesus foreknew several things. What were those things?
3. How does knowing God is all-powerful and all-knowing help you in your life?
4. Why do you think Peter objected to letting Jesus wash his feet? Why did Jesus say He must wash Peter's feet?
5. What was Jesus trying to teach them about how to serve one another?

Prayer

Lord, we do need to be washed clean of our sin. Thank you for making this possible. Nothing about Your suffering and death was a surprise to You but all part of God's plan to save the world. May trusting in Your control give us peace and confidence when we face difficult circumstances in our lives. May we learn from Your example of loving leadership and serve one another in humility. Amen.

Day 30 – Last Supper

Scripture – Luke 22:7-30; 1 Corinthians 5:7-8

Symbol – a cup

Songs – "Lamb of God," "Beautiful Redeemer," "The Present Value (Saved from death deserved...)"

Questions

1. What special meal were Jesus and His disciples celebrating?
2. What do you know about the importance of Passover?
3. According to Jesus, how were Peter and John to know where to prepare the meal?
4. What did Jesus say the bread and the cup symbolize?
5. Why do we celebrate communion?
6. In Luke 22:24-27, who did Jesus say is the greatest?
7. What do we learn about how we should exercise authority?
8. Read 1 Corinthians 5:7-8. Who is our Passover Lamb?

Prayer

Jesus, You are our Passover lamb. You died in our place, so that our sin would be passed over. Thank You for the new covenant in Your blood. May we remember Your great sacrifice each time we celebrate communion. May our lives be transformed by Your grace so that we follow Your example of service. Amen.

Day 31 – Gethsemane

Scripture – Mark 14:32-42
Symbol – a kneeling figure
Songs – "Hallelujah, What a Savior," "Tender Mercy"
Questions

1. Where did Jesus and the disciples go after the Passover Feast?

2. What did Jesus tell the disciples about how He was feeling?

3. How did Jesus respond to feeling distressed and troubled? How do you respond to feeling distressed and troubled?

4. What did Jesus pray? Are you able to submit to God's will when you are expecting something very difficult?

5. Why did Jesus rebuke the disciples? Why did they need prayer?

Prayer

Jesus, it is comforting to know that although You experienced trouble and distress during Your time on earth, You did not give in to temptation. Even though You knew exactly what was going to happen, You submitted to God's will. Help us to submit to Your will and cast our cares on You. Amen.

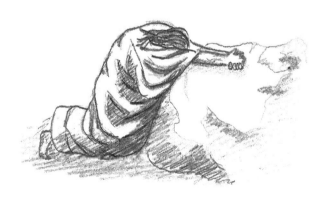

Day 32 – Jesus' Arrest

Scripture – Matthew 26:47-56; Romans 1:16

Symbol – kissing lips or a sword

Songs – "In All Your Ways Acknowledge Him," "Take My Life,"
   "Blessed Be Your Name," "Why?"

Questions

1. Who came with Judas to Gethsemane?
2. What was Judas' signal of whom to arrest? Have you ever outwardly been kind to someone while inwardly meaning them harm?
3. What did one of Jesus' companions do when men seized Him? How have you tried to handle circumstances without consulting God and without understanding?
4. What was His warning to His disciples about violence?
5. Who did Jesus indicate was in control?
6. Why did Jesus say these things must happen?
7. What did all the disciples do when Jesus was taken away?

Prayer

Lord, Your disciples who lived with You for three years had so little understanding of what you were about, and we are no different. Please forgive us when we betray, deny, abandon, fear, act in our own wisdom and strength, etc. Instead may we trust and rest in Your control, acknowledging You in all our ways. May we be like Paul who was able to say he was not ashamed of Your Gospel because it is Your power to save all who believe (Romans 1:16). Amen.

Day 33 – Peter's Denial

Scripture – Luke 22:31-34, 54-62; Psalm 103:8-12

Symbol – a rooster

Songs – "Grace Flows Down," "Arise, My Soul, Arise," "Greatest End," "The Shadow of Your Wings"

Questions

1. What warning did Jesus give Simon Peter? What did Jesus pray for Simon Peter? What did He tell Peter to do when he "turned back"?
2. What was Peter's vow? Have you ever had great intentions to follow Christ but fell short?
3. What was Jesus' prediction?
4. In Luke 22:54-62, how did Peter deny Christ?
5. What happened when he heard the rooster crow? How do you react when you see the ugliness of your sin?

Prayer

Lord, thank You for not being surprised by our failings, but offering forgiveness and restoration. Psalm 103:8-12 reassures us that You do not treat us according to what we deserve but that You are gracious and compassionate, removing our sins far from us. Give us strength to return, repent, and learn from our mistakes. Thank you for Peter's example of godly sorrow and repentance. Since You used him greatly to found Your church, we are hopeful that You will use us in Your kingdom despite our weaknesses. Amen.

Day 34 – Trial and Sentencing

Scripture – John 19:1-16, 23-25

Symbol – crown of thorns or dice

Songs – "Glorify Your Name (Father, I Adore You),"
  "Behold (the Lamb who was scorned...)

Questions

1. How did the soldiers treat Jesus? In what ways did Jesus suffer?
2. The soldiers mocked Him as king of the Jews. Do you consider Jesus a king; if so what is His kingdom?
3. Why did Pilate not want to kill Him? Why was Pilate afraid?
4. Why was it important that Jesus was innocent?
5. Pilate thought he had control over Jesus' fate, but how did Jesus respond?
6. Why did Pilate finally give in to the demands of Jewish leaders?
7. In John 19: 23-25, what did the soldiers do with Jesus' clothing? What does the passage say about why things had to happen this way?

Prayer

Jesus, You are the King of Kings! You deserve the honor and respect of all men. We are so grieved that You, being innocent and without sin, had to suffer beatings and insults for our sake. Heavenly Father, it is hard for us to understand that you ordained Christ's suffering, but we thank you for the detailed prophecies (Psalm 22:18, Isaiah 52:13-53:12, Psalm 34:20, Zechariah 12:10, etc.) that reveal and confirm your plan. Amen.

Day 35 – Crucifixion

Scripture – Matthew 27:32-56

Symbol – a cross

Songs – "When I Survey the Wondrous Cross," "Were You There?"

Questions

1. Where was Jesus crucified? Who was crucified with Him?
2. What insults were hurled at Him?
3. What happened for three hours while Jesus was dying?
4. What did Jesus cry out at the ninth hour? Why did He say this?
5. When Jesus died, what happened in the temple? This curtain separated the Holy of Holies from the rest of the temple. What is the significance of its tearing?
6. When these things happened, what did the centurion exclaim? Do you believe Jesus is the Son of God, who died to take away your sins?

Prayer

Jesus, we thank You for enduring humiliation, pain, separation from Your Father, and death to pay for our sin. We deserve death, but You took our punishment upon Yourself. All creation groaned at Your suffering: the sun was dark, the earth trembled, and godly people came back to life. Not only did You take our punishment, You also opened the way for us to be in relationship with our Heavenly Father, gave us eternal life, and clothed us in Your righteousness. You deserve all our praise and thanks. Amen.

Day 36 – Burial

Scripture – John 19:38-42; Matthew 27:57-66
Symbol – a tear drop or herbal sachet
Songs– "O Sacred Head, Now Wounded," "O the Deep, Deep Love
of Jesus," "Be Still and Know"

Questions

1. In John 19:38-42, who were the men who buried Jesus' body? These religious men could not celebrate the Passover that year because they had touched a dead body. What does this tell you about their love for Jesus?
2. How did they prepare His body for burial?
3. In Matthew 27:57-61, where was Christ's body placed?
4. Who was nearby watching? How would you have felt if you had been there?
5. In Matthew 27:62-66, what were the chief priests and Pharisees worried about?
6. What was done to protect Jesus' tomb?

Prayer

Lord, it is hard to imagine the grief of Your followers on the day of Your death, since they did not know what was coming on the third day. Like Joseph and Nicodemus may we show our love for You in tangible ways. May we give sacrificially of our time, energy, and resources to serve Your kingdom. Amen.

Day 37 – Resurrection

Scripture – Matthew 28:1-4; Luke 24:1-12; Philippians 3:10-11
Symbol – an empty tomb or shroud
Songs – "Christ the Lord is Risen Today," "Easter Song (Hear the Bells Ringing...)," "Christ Arose"

Questions

1. In Matthew 28:1-4, how was the tomb opened? What happened to the guards?
2. In Luke 24:1-12, who went to the tomb, and what did they find?
3. What were the women told about where Jesus had gone? What did the men remind the women that Jesus had said?
4. How did the disciples react to the women's story?
5. In Philippians 3:10-11, how does Paul react to Christ's resurrection? What is your reaction to Christ's resurrection?

Prayer

Lord, we greatly rejoice in Your resurrection! Because of Your resurrection we know that You have conquered sin and death. Wow, that is great news! Like the women who ran to tell the disciples the good news, may we look for opportunities to tell others about Jesus. Amen.

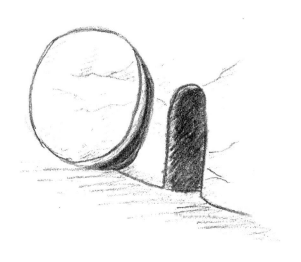

Day 38 – Appearing to Disciples

Scripture – John 20:19-31

Symbol – a hand with a scar

Songs – "Trust and Obey," "Behold, What Manner of Love,"
  "River of Fire"

Questions

1. What were the disciples doing at the beginning of this story?
2. How did Jesus greet them, and what did He show them?
3. What did He tell them to receive?
4. Who was missing, and how did he later respond to their story?
5. When Jesus came again, what did He tell Thomas?
6. Who did Jesus say are blessed?
7. Like Thomas, do you have trouble believing things you can't see?
8. Why did John write the Gospel of John? How may we have eternal life?

Prayer

Lord, help us to believe and not doubt, even though we don't see You in person. Thank You for the Bible, Your Word, that tells us about You so that we might believe. Thank You that Your gift of eternal life is available to all who simply believe. Give us faith to see and believe that Jesus is God and that He died to pay for our sins. Amen.

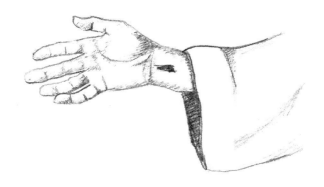

Day 39 – Miraculous Catch

Scripture – John 21:1-19

Symbol – a full net of fish

Songs – "I Love You, Lord," "Jesus Is all the World To Me," "Create In Me a Clean Heart," "There Is Joy In the Lord"

Questions

1. What were the disciples doing when Jesus appeared?
2. What did Jesus tell them to do and what happened?
3. How did Peter respond to the miracle?
4. What did Jesus ask Peter three times, and what instruction did He give Peter each time? Why do you think Jesus did this?
5. Despite Peter's denial and sin, his salvation was assured. Are you comforted by Christ's forgiveness and restoration of Peter?
6. What did Jesus predict? What final command did He give Peter?
7. What has God done in your life to build your faith?
8. Do you love Jesus? If you do, what does He want you to do?

Prayer

Lord, thank You for appearing to the disciples to build their faith. We pray that our faith would grow as we obey and follow You. Just as You forgave Peter for denying You and gave him the opportunity to affirm his love for You, thank You for forgiving us and giving us the chance to reaffirm our love for You and walk in obedience. Thank you that we can be confident in our salvation. Amen.

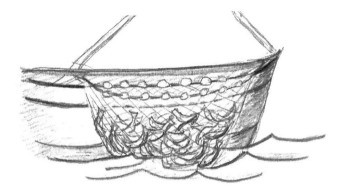

Day 40 – Ascension

Scripture – Acts 1:1-11

Symbol – a cloud

Songs – "Salvation Belongs to Our God," "Never Cease to Praise,"
*   "He is Exalted," "In Christ Alone," "Come, Christians, Join to Sing"*

Questions

1. For how many days after His resurrection did Jesus appear to the disciples before He ascended to heaven?
2. How did Jesus spend His time with them?
3. What did He tell them to do, and what did He promise? How will the Holy Spirit help them?
4. What did He say they would be when He was gone?
5. What happened to Jesus?
6. What did the men in white who appeared tell the disciples?
7. As Jesus' disciple, how can you be His witness in this world?
8. Who can you be praying for, and with whom can you be sharing the Good News about Jesus?

Prayer

Jesus, we look forward to Your return from heaven, but we know You have work for us to do now. Please give us a heart for the lost who don't know You. May we walk faithfully in the power of the Holy Spirit and have Your boldness to share Your truth with others. Amen.

Here is an additional idea for making your Easter celebration meaningful.

Easter Story Cookies (to be made the evening before Easter)
As you cook, explain the significance of the steps and read the scriptures.

Ingredients:
- 1 c. of pecans
- 1 tsp. of vinegar
- 3 egg whites
- Pinch of salt
- 1 c. sugar

Preheat oven to 300°F.
(This is important – don't wait until you are half done with recipe).

Place pecans in a zipper baggie and let children beat them with a wooden spoon into small pieces and set aside. *After Jesus was arrested He was beaten by the Roman soldiers (John 19:1-3).*

Let each child smell the vinegar. Put vinegar in mixing bowl. *When Jesus was thirsty on the cross He was given vinegar to drink (John 19:28-30).*

Add egg whites to vinegar. *Eggs represent life. Jesus gave His life to give us life (John 10:10-11).*

Sprinkle a little salt into each child's hand. Let them taste it and brush the rest into the bowl. *This represents the salty tears shed by Jesus' followers and the bitterness of our own sin (Luke 23:27).*

So far the ingredients are not very appetizing. Add 1 c. sugar. *The sweetest part of the story is that Jesus died because He loves us (Psalms 34:8 and John 3:16).*

Beat with a mixer on high speed for 12 to 15 minutes until stiff peaks form. *The color white represents how pure we look to God when our sins have been cleansed by Jesus (Isaiah 1:18 and 1 John 3:1-3).*

Fold in broken nuts. Drop by teaspoons onto a wax paper covered cookie sheet. *Each mound represents the rocky tomb where Jesus' body was laid (Matthew 27:57-60).*

Put the cookie sheet in the oven, close the door, and turn the oven OFF.

Give each child a piece of tape to seal the oven door. *Explain that Jesus' tomb was sealed (Matthew 27:65-66).*

Go to bed. *Explain that they feel sad to leave the cookies in the oven overnight. Jesus followers were in despair when the tomb was sealed (John 16:20-22).*

On Easter morning open the oven and give everyone a cookie. Notice the cracked surface and take a bite. The cookies are hollow! *On the first Easter Jesus' followers were amazed to find the tomb open and empty (Matthew 28:1-9).*

About the Author and Illustrator

Faye Nelson Maynard was born in The Democratic Republic of Congo to medical missionaries and lived there 7 years between the ages of birth and sixteen. She attended Vanderbilt University, where she graduated with a Bachelor's degree in Biology and a Masters in Science Education.

While her husband, Bill, was getting his medical training, she taught high school science for a couple of years. She loves being a wife and mother of two sons. Nashville, Tennessee is home for the Maynards, and they are members of Grace Community Church.

Throughout her life she has enjoyed creating beautiful things: paintings, photos, knitted items, quilts, etc. This project is such a joy because it has allowed her to use her artistic abilities to proclaim the Gospel. Her prayer is that the Lord Jesus would speak to your family through His Word and draw you closer to Him.

Lyrics for many of the suggested songs can be found at:
http://gccnashville.org/wp-content/uploads/2014/02/Lenten Songsheet.pdf

Made in the USA
Lexington, KY
10 March 2014